Daughter, you have always been
a wonderful source of joy to me.
You have touched my life
with a magic all your own...
I want you to know that the love we share
has made being a parent the greatest feeling
I have ever known.
— Deanna Beisser

Other Bestselling Blue Mountain Arts® Books

By Susan Polis Schutz:
To My Daughter, with Love, on the Important Things in Life
To My Son with Love
I Love You

100 Things to Always Remember... and One Thing to Never Forget
by Alin Austin

Is It Time to Make a Change?
by Deanna Beisser

Trust in Yourself
by Donna Fargo

To the One Person I Consider to Be My Soul Mate
by D. Pagels

For You, Just Because You're Very Special to Me
by Collin McCarty

Chasing Away the Clouds
by Douglas Pagels

Anthologies:
42 Gifts I'd Like to Give to You
Always Believe in Yourself and Your Dreams
Creeds of Life, Love, & Inspiration
Friends Are Forever
Friends for Life
I Love You, Mom
I'm Glad You Are My Sister
The Joys and Challenges of Motherhood
The Language of Recovery ... and Living Life One Day at a Time
Life Can Be Hard Sometimes ...but It's Going to Be Okay
Marriage Is a Promise of Love
Mottos to Live By
Take Each Day One Step at a Time
Teaching and Learning Are Lifelong Journeys
There Is Greatness Within You, My Son
These Are the Gifts I'd Like to Give to You
Think Positive Thoughts Every Day
Thoughts of Friendship
Thoughts to Share with a Wonderful Teenager
To My Child
True Friends Always Remain in Each Other's Heart
With God by Your Side ...You Never Have to Be Alone
Words of Love
You're Just like a Sister to Me

For You, My Daughter

...Poems to Say
How Much I Love You

A Special Blue Mountain Arts® Collection

Blue Mountain Press®

SPS Studios, Inc., Boulder, Colorado

Library of Congress Catalog Card Number: 00-011344
ISBN: 0-88396-572-0

Poems by Susan Polis Schutz appearing in this publication: Copyright © 1979, 1982, 1983, 1984, 1986, 1996 Stephen Schutz and Susan Polis Schutz. All rights reserved.

 Registered in the U.S. Patent and Trademark Office.
Certain trademarks are used under license.

Manufactured in China
First Printing: November 2000

This book is printed on recycled paper.

Library of Congress Cataloging-in-Publication Data

For you, my daughter : poems that say how much I love you: a special Blue Mountain Arts collection.
        p. cm.
    1. Mothers and daughters–Poetry. 2. Fathers and daughters–Poetry.
3. American poetry–20th century. 4. Daughters–Poetry. I. SPS Studios (Firm)
    PS595.M65 F67 2000
    811.008'03520441–dc21   00-011344
                                                            CIP

SPS Studios, Inc.
P.O. Box 4549, Boulder, Colorado 80306

Contents

Daughter, I Will Always Be Here with Love for You

Did you know that I loved you long before you were born?
When I first held you in my arms,
one of my childhood dreams came true.
I remember staring at your perfect little features
and feeling thrilled at each new sound and expression.
A fierce need to protect you came over me then,
and it has never gone away.
When you were a child,
I was able to hold you close through illness and heartache.
I could hold your hand as you faced new experiences,
and my presence and guidance seemed to
assure you of a certain level of safety.
But little by little, I have had to let you go
and allow you to make your own way.
So often I wanted to call you back and have you stay
in the protective circle of my arms.
I never wanted you to have to face injury or heartache,
yet I knew that you had to in order to grow.
Now you are making your own decisions.
Just remember that no matter what, I love you.
I could never stop loving you.
You are the hugs and smiles from my past,
the hopes and dreams of my future.
Take care, my daughter, and know that you are never alone.
We are connected by the strongest bond there is:
the love between parent and child.

– Barbara Cage

My Wish for You, Daughter

I can't give you the world,
filled with all its riches.
I can't promise you a life
free from sickness, pain,
and disappointment,
for that is a gift not mine to give.
I cannot guarantee that you
will never feel your heart break.
My only wish for you
is that you fulfill the dreams
deep within you...

I wish for you to know yourself
and be faithful to yourself.
For if you do,
you will be able to fully love others.
Be free to choose your course in life
without fearing a wrong decision.
Reflect on what you have been taught,
and take time to listen to your heart.
Never lose the ability to feel with open arms
all the passion and joy that life holds for you.
Give all you have
without looking for something in return.
Reach out for that which you can attain
and not for that which is impossible.
I wish for you, my daughter,
to be all you can,
for only then will you awaken
to the person you want to be.

— Joan Benicken

When you are happy,
  I'll love you with
    a joyful heart.
When you are sad,
  I'll love you with a heart
    made a little heavier
      by your tears.
When you are right,
  I'll love you with a heart
    filled with pride.
When you are wrong,
  I'll love you with a heart
    that has learned acceptance.
When you succeed,
  I'll love you with
    a cheering heart.
When you fail,
  I'll love you with a heart
    that rewards the efforts you've made.
When you dream,
  I'll love you with
    an encouraging heart.
When you give up,
  I'll love you with a heart
    that is strong enough for both of us.
When you are simply you,
in whatever mood or phase of your life,
  I'll love you with all my heart
    and more than you'll ever know.

– Linda Sackett-Morrison

To My Daughter,
I Love You

When you were born
I held you in my arms
and just kept smiling at you
You always smiled back
your big eyes wide open
full of love
You were such a
beautiful
good
sweet baby
Now
as I watch you grow up
and become your own person
I look at you
your laughter
your happiness
your simplicity
your beauty

And I know that you will
be able to enjoy a life
of sensitivity
goodness
accomplishment
and love
in a world that hopefully is at peace
I want to tell you that
I am so proud of you
and I dearly
love you

— Susan Polis Schutz

Daughter,
I Want You to Know…

It's hard sometimes, when people
are changing their lives, to
understand each other, or even
to talk. You are struggling right
now for independence and the
right to live your own way…
and I sometimes struggle for
the strength to let you do it.
I wish now and then for the days
when a kiss or a hug could make
your world bright again; but
your world is more difficult now,
and you want to make your own
way in it — which is as it should be.
I only want you to know…
that when you get hurt, I will
hurt for you; and that deep
down, I always have confidence
in your ability to find your place
in your world. If you ever need a
caring heart, or someone to listen
to your deepest dreams or concerns,
I will be there for you;
and remember, above all else…
that I love and care for you.

— M. Joye

You're a Very Special Person

Carry the sun inside you,
and reach out for the dreams that guide you.
You have everything you need to take
you where you want to go.
You have abilities and talents
and attributes that belong to you alone,
and you have what it takes to make
your path of success... lead to happiness.

You're a very special person.
You have qualities that get better every day!
You have the courage and strength to see
*   things through.*
You have smiles that will serve as your guides.
You have a light that will shine in you
*   'til the end of time.*
You have known the truth of yesterday,
*   and you have an inner map that will*
*   lead the way to a very beautiful tomorrow.*
You have gifts that have never even been opened
*   and personal journeys waiting to be explored.*
You have so much going for you.
You are a special person, and you have a
*   future that is in the best of hands.*
*   And you need to remember: If you have*
*   plans you want to act on and dreams*
*   you've always wanted to come true...*

You have what it takes, because...
*   You*
*   have*
*   you.*

— Douglas Pagels

Did you know,
  sweet daughter of mine,
That my world changed forever
When you came into my life?
No one could have prepared me
  for the depth of love
That sprang into my heart for you
From the very moment you were born.
And I continually think of ways
  I can let you know
How very special you are to me.
You truly are a treasure,
And I will cherish you all of my life.
I will brag about you and show you off
Every time I get the chance.
And though I don't know how
  it's possible,
You become more dear to me
With every year that passes by.

— Cheryl Barker

In Case I Haven't Told You Lately...

Many days go by and I find myself saying
the same things to you day in and day out:
"Clean your room."
"Is your room clean?"
"Do your homework."
"Did you finish your homework?"
"Don't be late."
"Take the trash out, please..."

Many nights, after you have
fallen asleep and look so peaceful,
I have wondered to myself...
Did I tell you that I love you?
That I appreciate all you do for me?
That through your entire life
you will find me in your cheering section?
Have I asked you lately about your happiness
and what's going on in your life?

I am sorry that there are so many times
when I get caught up with the everyday routines
that I forget the simple, important things in life.
I hope that you will forgive me for my shortcomings,
as I will forgive you.
Always remember that
no matter how busy I seem to be,
I love you very much,
and I am proud of all that you do
and all that you stand for.

— Toni Crossgrove Shippen

$\mathcal{D}$aughter, you have always been
a wonderful source of joy to me.
You have touched my life
with a magic all your own.
There were times when you struggled with me,
longing for your own independence
and searching for your own place in the world.
I remember those times as
I tried to hold you close
and hold on tightly to my little girl,
knowing all the time in my heart that
it was a part of growing up for you and for me,
a part of life we would endure
and eventually become closer than ever before.
You are more than a dream come true for me:
you are a part of my life that will carry on.
And as I watch you changing,
I see a special happiness in all that you do.
With my heart full of memories,
I want you to know that the love we share
has made being a parent the greatest feeling
I have ever known.

— Deanna Beisser

I hope that today
    and always
the love I have for you
is reaching out
and touching you –
    making your days
        a little brighter
    and your heart
        a little warmer.

I hope that today
    and always
you are aware of how
special you are to me,
and how lucky I feel
    to have you in my life.

— Susie Schneider

I ask myself
    why I have been
        blessed with someone
        so understanding
        and so caring...
    Perhaps it's because
    I can truly appreciate you
    or maybe it's because
        God knew
        I needed you
        so much.

— Jean Therese Lynch

May There Always Be Happiness in Your Life

*Happiness cannot come from without.
It must come from within. It is not what we
see and touch or that which others do for us
which makes us happy; it is that which we
think and feel and do, first for the other
fellow and then for ourselves.*

— Helen Keller

*Keep
your face to
    the sunshine
and you cannot
    see the shadow.*

— Helen Keller

Don't Ever...

Don't ever try to understand everything –
some things will just never make sense.
Don't ever be reluctant to show your feelings –
when you're happy, give in to it!
When you're not, live with it.
Don't ever be afraid to try to make things better –
you might be surprised at the results.
Don't ever take the weight of the world
on your shoulders.
Don't ever feel threatened by the future –
take life one day at a time.
Don't ever feel guilty about the past –
what's done is done. Learn from any mistakes
you might have made.
Don't ever feel that you are alone –
there is always somebody there for you
to reach out to.
Don't ever forget that you can achieve
so many of the things you can imagine –
imagine that! It's not as hard as it seems.
Don't ever stop loving,
don't ever stop believing,
don't ever stop dreaming your dreams.

– Laine Parsons

My Dear Daughter...

I know I am critical of you sometimes, but it's only because I have experienced so much more of life, and I can often see that the path you are taking today may not take you to where you want to be tomorrow.

I know, too, that you still have to experience life for yourself. If I can, I just want to spare you some of the pain I had to go through on my own path in life...

When the words don't come with all I want to say, I can still say this: I love you tremendously. I would do anything for you. And I promise I will try to be more patient and understanding of you, and I pray that you will do the same for me.

And do me a favor sometimes... tell me you love me, okay? Having you grow up so quickly is hard on me.

– Carol Ann Bader

It's Up to You to Make Your Life the Best It Can Be

This life is the only one you're given.
Look for opportunities to grow,
and never be discouraged
in your efforts to do so.
Replace your weaknesses with positives;
take life's broken pieces
and re-create your dreams.
Never measure the future by the past;
let yesterday become a memory
and tomorrow a promise.
Begin each day by focusing
on all that is good,
and you'll be in a position
to handle whatever comes along.
Take responsibility for your actions;
never make excuses
for not being the best you can be.
If you should slip,
be comforted by the thought
that we all do at times.
Determine your tomorrow
by the choices you make today,
and you'll find yourself living
in joy and triumph.

— Linda E. Knight

Whenever Life Is Getting You Down, Daughter, Remember This...

To solve each problem one at a time;
to take each day as it comes.
To stick to your goals, no matter
        what happens,
and press on toward your dreams.
To keep your attention focused on
        the future,
as you consider the solutions at hand.
To look for the bright side,
even though it may be temporarily
        covered by a cloud.
To smile often, even when a frown
        feels more natural.
To think of those you love,
        and know that they love you, too.

No matter how difficult it may seem,
you have within you the power,
        the ability,
                and the knowledge
        to make things better.

– Lindsay Newman

*Y*our life can be
   what you want it to be...
You'll make it through
   whatever comes along.

Within you are so many answers.
   Understand, have courage,
      be strong.
                    – Douglas Pagels

*W*hen you encounter difficulties and
contradictions, do not try to break
them, but bend them with gentleness
and time.
                    – St. Francis de Sales

Daughter, You Are Loved

When the road seems too long
When darkness sets in
When everything turns out wrong
And you can't find a friend
Remember - you are loved

When smiles are hard to come by
And you're feeling down
When you spread your wings to fly
And can't get off the ground
Remember - you are loved

When time runs out before you're through
And it's over before you begin
When little things get to you
And you just can't win
Remember - you are loved

When your loved ones are far away
And you are on your own
When you don't know what to say
When you're afraid of being alone
Remember – you are loved

When your sadness comes to an end
And everything is going right
May you think of your family and friends
And keep their love in sight
A thank-you for being loved

May you see the love around you
In everything you do
And when troubles seem to surround you
May all the love shine through
You are blessed – you are loved

– Roger Pinches

Daughter, Your Happiness Is What I Wish for Most

I wish for you to always see the goodness
in this world,
to do your part in helping those
less fortunate,
to walk hand in hand with those
of less talent,
to follow those of more knowledge,
to be an equal with those who are different.

I wish for you to find your special purpose
in this world so full of choices
and to help lead those who stray.
I wish for you to become your own
individual, to set yourself apart from
those who are the same.

I wish for you the self-confidence
to say no when it is necessary
and the strength to stand alone.

*I wish for you the approval of yourself
  to love and respect everything that
    you are and will become.
I wish for you to reap the fruits
  of your talents,
to walk with pride down the road of life,
to be humble in your successes,
and to share in the praises and joy
  of others.
But most of all,
I wish for you to be happy.
For when you are happy,
  you have the key that will open all
    of the world's doors to you.*

*Whatever you decide,
  whoever you become,
my love for you is unconditional;
my arms and heart are always open to you.
My wishes for you are that you will someday
  know the joys that only a daughter
    can bring
and that all your wishes come true.
I love you, my daughter.*

                              – Jackie Olson

Daughter, You Are Special

Within you is an ideal,
a voice of youth,
and a promise of achievement
still to come.
Within your hands
are special gifts and talents.
Within your mind is the
source of your dreams.
Within you is the strength
to carry your dreams to completion.
Within your heart is the desire
to meet the world on your own terms.
You are strong; you are wise;
you have a dream.
You have a spirit and confidence;
you have faith.
You are your own person,
and you always will be.
Within you is something
so precious and rare.
Within you is the promise
of the future.

– Jean Lamey

*"Special" is a word
that is used to describe
something one-of-a-kind
like a hug
or a sunset
or a person who spreads love
with a smile or kind gesture.
"Special" describes people
who act from the heart
and keep in mind the hearts
   of others.
"Special" applies to something
that is admired and precious
and which can never be replaced.
"Special" is the word that best
   describes you.*

                                    – Teri Fernandez

Daughter...

If ever you need to talk,
to share a laugh,
a dream, a smile;
to be comforted
or reassured,
to be understood...

Remember,
my shoulder is there
for your head,
your secrets are safe
and my door
is always open.

– Ronda Scott

I am always here
to understand you
I am always here
to laugh with you
I am always here
to cry with you
I am always here
to talk to you
I am always here
to think with you
I am always here
to plan with you
Even though we
might not always
be together
please know that
I am always
here to
love
you

– Susan Polis Schutz

Remember This, My Daughter...

There is no difficulty that enough love will not conquer; No disease that enough love will not heal; No door that enough love will not open; No gulf that enough love will not bridge; No wall that enough love will not throw down; No sin that enough love will not redeem...

It makes no difference how deeply seated may be the trouble; How hopeless the outlook; How muddled the tangle; How great the mistake. A sufficient realization of love will dissolve it all... If only you could love enough you would be the happiest and most powerful being in the world.

– Emmet Fox

Your success and happiness lie in you. External conditions are the accidents of life, its outer trappings. The great, enduring realities are love of service. Joy is the holy fire that keeps our purpose warm and our intelligence aglow. Resolve to keep happy, and your joy and you shall form an invincible host against difficulty.

– Helen Keller

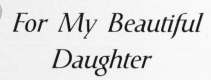

For My Beautiful Daughter

I looked at you today
and saw the same beautiful eyes
that looked at me with love
when you were a baby
I looked at you today
and saw the same
   beautiful mouth
that made me cry
   when you first smiled at me
when you were a baby
It was not long ago
that I held you in my arms
long after you fell asleep
and I just kept rocking you
all night long

*I looked at you today
and saw my beautiful daughter
no longer a baby
but a beautiful person
with a full range of emotions
    and feelings
and ideas and goals
Every day is exciting
as I continue to watch you grow
And I want you to always know that
in good and in bad times
I will love you
and that no matter what you do
or how you think
or what you say
you can depend on
my support, guidance
friendship and love
every minute of every day
I love being your mother*

– Susan Polis Schutz

Some Special Wishes
Just for You

Wishing you a message
   of how special you are.
Today. Tomorrow. And forever.
Wishing you days of celebration.
And favorite people gathered together.

Wishing you wonderful thoughts.
And the best memories anybody ever had.
Wishing you new paths and promises ahead.
And a million reasons to be glad.

Wishing you the warmth of friends and family.
And loved ones always close by.
Wishing you the gifts happiness brings.
And the treasures money can't buy.

Wishing you success and serenity.
And wishes come true.
Wishing you a reminder of how much nicer
   this world is... because of you.

— Casey Whilson

Daughter, You Are the Most Beautiful Flower in the Garden of My Life

Like a flower whose petals
unfold before my eyes,
I watch as you reach out
to grab hold of
the new opportunities
that are coming your way.
My little flower…
I hope you have been listening
to all the things
I have tried so hard
to impress upon you.
Changes and challenges
have presented themselves…
and you stand ready for anything.

Pride is what I feel
for this precious flower,
as I watch you blossom
into a beautiful young woman.
You have learned to dream,
but more importantly,
you have learned to strive
toward your goals.
You are strong and independent
and more beautiful
than any flower I have ever seen.

– Karen G. Osman

A Daughter Is a
Wonderful Blessing

*A daughter is one of the greatest
    blessings one could ever have
She begins her life loving and
    trusting you automatically*

*And for many years, you are
    the center of her life
Together you experience the
    delights of the new things
    she learns and does*

*You enter into a daughter's play and are once
    again young
And even though it's harder to enter into her
    world as she becomes a teen*

*You are there, understanding her dilemmas and
    her fears
And wishing with all your heart that she didn't
    have to go through them*

*A daughter's smile is a precious sight that
    you treasure each time you see it
And the sound of her laughter always brings
    joy to your heart*

Her successes mean more to you than your own
And her happiness is your happiness

Her heartaches and disappointments
*   become yours, too*
Because when she isn't okay, you can't
*   be okay either*

Daughters aren't perfect, but you come
*   close to it*
You have given me more happiness
*   than you know*

I am thankful for your kindness and
*   thoughtfulness*
And I am proud of who you are
*   and how you live your life*

Words can't express how much you mean
*   to me or how much I love you*
The love goes too deep, and the gratitude
*   and pride I feel are boundless*

Thank you, Daughter, for blessing
*   my life in so many ways*

– Barbara Cage

$\mathcal{I}$ want you to know how amazing you are.
I want you to know how much you're
treasured and celebrated and quietly thanked.

I want you to feel really good... about who you are.
About all the great things you do!
I want you to appreciate your uniqueness.
Acknowledge your talents and abilities.
Realize what a beautiful soul you have.
Understand the wonder within.

You make so much sun shine through, and you
inspire so much joy in the lives of everyone who is
lucky enough to know you.

You are a very special person, giving so many
people a reason to smile. You deserve to receive the
best in return, and one of my heart's favorite
hopes is that the happiness you give away will
come back to warm you
          each and every day of your life.

— Sydney Nealson

Always Believe
in Yourself, Daughter
...and Know That You Are Loved

Know yourself –
what you can do
and want to do in life
Set goals
and work hard to achieve them
Have fun every day in every way
Be creative –
it is an expression of your feelings
Be sensitive in viewing the world
Believe in the family
as a stable and rewarding way
of life
Believe in love
as the most complete
and important emotion possible
Believe that you are
an important part of
everyone's life that you touch
Believe in yourself
and know that you are loved

– Susan Polis Schutz

Fathers and Daughters...

When a father looks upon a daughter he bears the love that he bore her mother echoed down through the years.

— Thomas Moore

Certain it is that there is no kind of affection so purely angelic as that of a father to a daughter. He beholds her both with and without regard to her sex. In love to our wives there is desire; to our sons there is ambition; but in that to our daughters there is something which there are no words to express.

— Joseph Addison

The lucky man has a daughter as his first child.

— Spanish Proverb

Mothers and Daughters...

*M*others *of daughters*
are daughters of mothers
and have remained so, in
circles joined to circles,
since time began. They
are bound together by
a shared destiny.

– *Signe Hammer*

*T*hou *art thy mother's glass, and she in thee*
Calls back the lovely April of her prime.

– *William Shakespeare*

*L*ike *one, like the other*
Like daughter, like mother.

– *Anonymous*

A Family's Love Can Rise Above Anything That Comes Along

My dear and wonderful daughter,
we all have times
when it seems like
the sun forgot to shine in our lives
and the dreams we were counting
so heavily on... forgot how much
we wanted them to come true.

When you need a place of comfort,
a hand to hold, and a heart that cares
about your happiness more than words
can ever say... remember that you can
turn to me... and I'll do whatever
I can to help you
*   chase those clouds away.*

– Ann Turrel

I Am Always Here for You, Daughter...

When you need someone
to talk to
I hope you will
talk to me
When you need someone
to laugh with
I hope you will
laugh with me
When you need someone
to advise you
I hope you will
turn to me
When you need someone
to help you
I hope you will
let me help you
I cherish and love
everything about you –
my beautiful daughter
And I will always support you
as a mother, as a person
and as a friend

— Susan Polis Schutz

My Advice
to You, Daughter...

Enjoy your life!
Laugh a lot. Love a lot.
Listen to your heart,
and follow where it leads you.
Do what you love.
Love yourself,
and share that love with others.
This is the way that we truly
make a difference,
add our beauty to the world,
and give something precious
to ourselves and others.
You have already
made an impression on the world.
You have touched my heart
and my life
in a way that has
forever changed me.
Thank you for coming into my life,
for forgiving any errors I made
in raising you,
and for allowing me the chance
to learn and grow with you.
I love you.

— Donna Newman

Do all the good you can,
By all the means you can,
In all the ways you can,
In all the places you can,
At all the times you can,
To all the people you can,
As long as ever you can.

— John Wesley

Finish every day and be done with it. For manners and for wise living it is a vice to remember. You have done what you could; some blunders and absurdities no doubt crept in; forget them as soon as you can. To-morrow is a new day; you shall begin it well and serenely, and with too high a spirit to be cumbered with your old nonsense. This day for all that is good and fair. It is too dear, with its hopes and invitations, to waste a moment on... yesterdays.

— Ralph Waldo Emerson
(From a letter to his daughter)

Always remember to forget
the things that made you sad,
but never forget to remember
the things that made you glad.

— Elbert Hubbard

Daughter, You Are the Greatest Gift I've Ever Received

*Memories come
flooding back to me
    as I look back
        over the years.
I want to hold on to you
and at the same time
watch you fly high and free.*

*You have such spirit
    and a character all your own.
You are a doer and an achiever
    of what you believe in.
I'm so proud of your dreams
    and the conviction you have
to make those dreams come true.
Your world is bright, new,
    and bursting with possibilities.*

It's so easy to remember
   your very first steps
and how I held out my hand
   for you to hold.

As each year passes,
   you take more steps,
and some of these will eventually
   lead you away from me –
but always remember that
   my hand and my heart
      are forever here for you.
You will always be my daughter,
   but I have also discovered in you
a rare and precious friend.
You have been life's greatest gift
   to me,
and I love you so much.

– Vickie M. Worsham

You have powers you never dreamed of. *You can do things you never thought you could do. There are no limitations in what you can do except the limitations in your own mind as to what you cannot do.*

Don't think you cannot.

Think you can.

— *Darwin P. Kingsley*

I will support you
in all that you
do
I will help you
in all that you
need
I will share with you
in all that you
experience
I will encourage you
in all that you
try
I will understand you
in all that is in your
heart
I will love you
in all that you
are

— Susan Polis Schutz

Gentle Words
of Encouragement

Spend every day preparing for the next.

*As you reach forward with one hand, accept
the advice of those who have gone before
you, and in the same manner reach back
with the other hand to those who follow
you; for life is a fragile chain of experiences
held together by love. Take pride in being a
strong link in that chain. Discipline yourself,
but do not be harsh. The pleasures of life are
yours to be taken. Share them with others,
but always remember that you, too, have
earned the right to partake.*

Know those who love you; love is the finest
of all gifts and is received only to be
given. Embrace those who truly love
you; for they are few in a lifetime.
Then return that love tenfold, radiating it
from your heart to fill their lives as
sunlight warms the darkest corners of the
earth. Love is a journey, not a destination;
travel its path daily. Do this and your
troubles will be as fleeting as footprints
in the sand. When loneliness is your
companion and all about you seem to be
gone, pause and listen, for the sound of
loneliness is silence, and in silence we
hear best. Listen well, and your
moments of silence will always be
broken by the gentle words of
encouragement spoken by those of us
who love you.

– Tim Murtaugh

My Family

There is an
irreplaceable feeling
that I wouldn't give up for the world –
a sense of belonging,
of being able to turn
to the outstretched hands
*   of those I love... at any time;*
to know they'll understand me,
*   and comfort me*
*   when things go wrong,*
or laugh with me
*   when things make me happy.*
Caring and sharing
*   life's ups and downs,*
and mostly,
*   loving...*
as I so dearly love them.

– Debbie Avery Pirus

The family is one of
*   nature's masterpieces.*

– George Santayana

You are my daughter, and the meaning of
   that bond between us is boundless.
It means placing your comfort before my own.
It means trying my best every moment of
   every day to shelter you from harm.
It means worrying endlessly, and sometimes
   needlessly, about you and everything that
   enters your life.
It means wanting only the best for you, and
   aching inside at those times when things
   go wrong.
It means giving you all that I have to give
   and feeling your special love fill my
   heart more deeply than I ever imagined.
It means loving you without reserve, and
   with all that I am, for the rest of my life.

– Linda Sackett-Morrison

*D*ear Daughter,

I worry sometimes that I pushed
* too hard*
when you were growing up –
wanting so much for you
and trying to make sure you had
all those things that I didn't
* when I was a child.*
But I hope that I never made you
feel that I expected too much...
for no matter what you become
* or what you achieve,*
what matters most to me is that
* you're happy*
and that I'm never without your
* love.*

I'll always be here for you...
* no matter what you do.*

– Anna Marie Edwards

*It is so important
to choose your own
lifestyle
and not let others
choose it for you*

– Susan Polis Schutz

*Do not follow where
the path may lead.
Go, instead, where
there is no path
and leave a trail.*

– Anonymous

Hold Fast Your Dreams

Hold fast your dreams!
Within your heart
Keep one still, secret spot
Where dreams may go,
And, sheltered so,
May thrive and grow
Where doubt and fear are not.
O keep a place apart,
Within your heart,
For little dreams to go!

Think still of lovely things that are not true.
Let wish and magic work at will in you.
Be sometimes blind to sorrow. Make believe!
Forget the calm that lies
In disillusioned eyes.
Though we all know that we must die,
Yet you and I
May walk like gods and be
Even now at home in immortality.

We see so many ugly things –
Deceits and wrongs and quarrelings;
We know, alas! we know
How quickly fade
The color in the west,
The bloom upon the flower,
The bloom upon the breast
And youth's blind hour.
Yet keep within your heart
A place apart
Where little dreams may go,
May thrive and grow.
Hold fast – hold fast your dreams!

– Louise Driscoll

When the world closes in
and lies so heavily upon you...
remember that I care.
When the ones with whom you
share your life seem like strangers...
remember that I care.
When love seems to only bring
you pain...
remember that I care.
What cannot be, cannot be.
But always remember, I care.
Never be afraid to come to me,
if you have need of the
*   simplest thing.*
No matter what it is...
*   I care.*

– Kathy Boss

i wish for you warmth
when it is cold outside

i wish for you a star
when the night is dark

i wish for you courage
when the world is afraid

i think of you, i wish for you
and i hope you know –
that here, there is a heart
and a home;
and here, there is someone
who loves you
more than any wish could
        ever give.

        – laura west rosenthal

Child of Mine

It's been so gratifying
for me to see you
go through such positive changes
*   and inner growth.*
Your happiness is contagious,
*   and I'm so happy for you...*
to see you becoming
*   a strong individual*
and doing all the right things
to make your days ahead
*   shine even brighter.*

It's been great for me
to watch you grow
and to become
even more of that special someone
*   you are... inside.*

Through your growing and changing,
I want to ask that you
   take me along with you.
I don't mean that I want you
to tell me every thought
   you have along the way,
but to remember that I am here...
   wherever and whenever you need me.
And I hope that you'll remember
   that I'm on your side.
And even if I can't always help you win,
there will never be a day
   when I won't be
         cheering you on.

– Laine Parsons

My darling daughter
I am so glad that
you were born today
when women are so
aware of what is going on
and don't always have
to fight so hard to be heard
The world is wide open
for you to be whatever you want
It will be hard
but at least you
will find other women
striving for the same things
and you won't be called "crazy"
for wanting to achieve them
Though full equality
is a long way off
there certainly have been changes
which would make your life as a woman
not so stereotyped and confined
My darling daughter
you are living in an age
where womanhood is finally growing
to be everything
that it can be

— Susan Polis Schutz

Believe in Yourself, and Live Your Life with Thankfulness for All the Gifts You've Been Given

You have the ability to become
all you are capable
of becoming.
Forget problems
that don't matter anymore
and worries that will wash away
on the shore of tomorrow.
Determine your own worth
by yourself,
and do not be dependent
on another's judgment of you.
Dare to dream,
and live those dreams,
for it is then
that you can begin to realize
your true destiny.
Live life fully
with thankfulness and joy
for all the gifts
you've been given.

– Debbi Oehman

More Than You Know...
Daughter

I'd like to tell you
how much I love you,
and I hope you know that I do...
I wish that the words I speak
*   so gently to you could be*
heard by your heart
*   with the same meanings*
and the same soft feelings of love
that they carry from deep within me.

For more than you know...
*   I love so many things about you.*
*   I enjoy sharing life with you.*
I enjoy the way we balance each other out,
how we share the good times
*   and support each other through the tears...*

I enjoy the knowledge that we'll make it
   through whatever life brings
with courage and with love
through the years.

More than you know...
   and more than I can ever say,
I feel a wonderful thankfulness
   in my heart... just for you.
And I want you to remember, though
   my thoughts don't always convey
   and my feelings don't always show,
I love you, and I always will...
   more than you know.

                          – Andrew Tawney

I'm Fortunate to Have a Daughter Who Is Also My Friend

You must know that I love you
and that I am proud you are my daughter,
but I may have failed to let you know
how I feel about you as a person.
When you were young, it seemed as if
I was constantly busy taking care of you
and trying to keep up with
the demands of raising a child.
Yet you were always my greatest joy.
In time, it seemed as if our roles somehow became reversed,
and you returned my devotion
by letting me lean on you.
There were times when you seemed
so wise for your years
that I caught a glimpse of the woman
you would someday become.
Now you are that woman,
and I'm proud that you are my daughter.
But you are also a very special person
who has filled my life with a precious, ever-growing friendship.
You are my dearest friend –
one who is loving, kind, and compassionate.
You support me at all times by giving your time and love;
I know I can count on you to always be there.
You listen to my problems
with quiet understanding, and through you
I am often able to find solutions.
You are my biggest fan
when I have achieved a personal goal,
sharing my triumphs with pride and affection.
I love you because you are my daughter,
but I also love you for the very special person you are.

— Lori Pike

I Think of You
Every Day

You probably don't realize how important you are to me. There are times when the one thing that helps me get through the day... is thinking of you.

You bring happiness to me when the world seems to be wearing a frown. When things don't quite go as planned and my world seems upside down, my thoughts of you help to set things right again.

You are so important to me.
You make me think, you make me laugh, you make me feel alive. You put things in perspective for me. You provide support and encouragement, you lessen my worries, and you increase my joys. If my life were a puzzle, you would be the one piece that was a perfect fit.

Every day... I think of you.
And I've got a million smiles to prove it.

— Marin McKay

Daughter, You Are So Precious to Me

When you came into this world and into my life, so many beautiful things happened. Although I was the one holding you, you were the one enfolding so many of my hopes and dreams. Although I was the one who was supposed to teach you all the things to do as you grew up, you were the one who taught me — constantly — of my capacity to love, to experience life in its most meaningful way, and to open my heart wide enough to let all those joyful feelings inside.

If ever you wonder if anyone cares, know that the love I have for you transcends time and bridges any distance imaginable. Remember: If you ever need me, I will <u>always</u> be there... Nothing will ever be as strong as my love and my thankfulness... for you.

— Laurel Atherton

*Even
if a day
should go by
when I don't say
"I love you..."*

*May never a
moment go by
without you
knowing I do*

– Daniel Haughian

A Wish for You,
My Daughter

*If there could be only one thing
in life for me to teach you,
I would teach you to love...*

*To respect others so that you may
find respect in yourself
To learn the value of giving,
so that if ever there comes a time
in your life when someone is really in
need, you will give
To act in a manner that you would
wish to be treated; to be proud
of yourself
To laugh and smile as much as you
can, in order to help bring joy
back into this world
To have faith in others;
to be understanding
To stand tall in this world and
to learn to depend on yourself*

*To only take from this earth
those things which you really
need, so there will be enough
for others
To not depend on money or
material things for your
happiness, but
To learn to appreciate the people
who love you, the simple beauty
that God gave you and to find
peace and security within
yourself*

*To you, my child, I hope I have
taught all of these things,
for they are love.*

– Donna Dargis

To My Daughter

Since you were born
you have been
such a beautiful
addition to our family
Now that you are growing up
I can see that
you are a beautiful
addition to the world
and I am so
proud of you

As we watch you
doing things on your own
we know you will find
happiness and success
because we are confident in
your ability
your self-knowledge
your values
But if you ever need a boost
or just someone to talk to
about difficulties that might be occurring
we are always here
to help you
to understand you
to support you
and to love
you

        – Susan Polis Schutz

Daughter

*Goals are dreams and wishes
that are not easily reached.
You have to work hard to
obtain them,
never knowing when
or where
you will reach your goal.*

*But keep trying!
Do not give up hope.
And most of all…
never stop
believing in yourself.*

*For within you
there is someone
special…*

*someone wonderful
and successful.
No matter what you achieve,
as long as you want it
and it makes you
happy,*

you are a success.

– Rosemary DePaolis

My Darling Daughter

You are a shining
example of what a
daughter can be –
love and laughter
beautiful and good
honest and principled
determined and independent
sensitive and intelligent
You are a shining
example of what every
mother wishes her
daughter were
and I
am so very
proud of
you

– Susan Polis Schutz

Daughter,
You Have Given Me
Happiness and Smiles

You are a blessing
that I'm forever thankful for.
I love being with you,
and every time we're apart
there's a little part of me
that stays with you.

Your sense of humor delights me.
Your laughter is one of
    my favorite sounds,
and your smiles light up my heart.

I'm so proud of you
and the kind of person you are.
People know they can count on you.
You go out of your way for others
and make a difference in the lives
    of those you care about.
You're helpful to others,
and you are independent, as well.
I'm very pleased with all
you've accomplished on your own.

I love you,
and I want you to know
that being your parent
has been one of my greatest joys.

– Barbara Cage

Carry This Thought in Your Heart Forever...

*If I could stand beside you always,
I would.
If I could carry you over all the obstacles,
I would.
If I could turn all your tears to laughter,
I would.
If I could tell you
all that will happen to you,
I would.
But I can only tell you
one thing with certainty:
I love you.
And I hope my love will
shine on all your tomorrows
and brighten every step
you take in the future.*

— Dorothy Hewitt